Civic Adventures

How Individuals, Families, and Communities Learn Together

Shawntel D. Carey, MPA

SDC Compass Publishing LLC

Civic Adventures:
How Individuals, Families, and Communities Learn Together

Written by Shawntel D. Carey, MPA

Copyright © 2025 SDC Compass Publishing LLC

All rights reserved

No part of this publication may be reproduced or transmitted in any form or by any means, electronic or mechanical, including photocopying, recording, or by any information storage and retrieval system, without written permission from the publisher, except in the case of brief quotations embodied in critical articles or reviews.

Published by SDC Compass Publishing LLC
Lawrenceville, Georgia

Interior and illustrations created in collaboration with aicisssistedshkingllc@gmail.com

Printed in the United States of America

Print ISBN: 979-8-9939033-1-6
eBook ISBN: 979-8-9939033-0-9

For the families
who learn together,
lead together,
and lift their communities
every day.

Author's Note

This book was written with families like yours in mind. I believe learning and understanding civics is important for all ages. It can shape how we see the world and our role in it. By reading this book with children, you have already taken a positive step forward. Small acts of service like the ones shown in this book can strengthen our communities and become building blocks for lasting involvement. I hope this book helps inspire new ways of seeing yourself as an important part of your community.

Welcome to Civic Adventures

First, there's local government! That's how our city or town is run. The mayor and other leaders work on things like parks and libraries. Let's meet them!

How to Contact Your Local Government

These are some of the typical departments in local government

Clerk's Department **Department of Public Works**
Economic Development **Health Department**
Planning & Zoning **Code Enforcement**
Parks & Recreation **Fire Department**

How to find them:
1. Visit your city or county website.
2. Look for 'department' or office that interests you most

I want to learn more about this area of my local government because_____

Does this area of my local government offer tours?
(If so, plan another field with your family and friends)

MEET YOUR LOCAL LEADERS

Name:	Contact Info (Phone/Email/ Social)

Something Interesting I Learned

Our Local Leaders

Today, our family visited City Hall to learn about how our local government works.

A city worker welcomed us inside. "We make decisions that help our community." she said.

Who fixes the potholes?

Sort each job into Local or Not Local.

Local	Not Local
 **Mayor**	 **Governor**
 **City Council/ Commissioner**	 **School Board Member**

Our State Leaders

Today, our family visited our state capitol to learn about how state government works.

A state worker showed us the place where laws are made. We learned about the state level!

How to Contact Your State Government

To find information about your state capital
https://www.usa.gov/elected-officials

Find your State and territorial elected officials
https://www.usa.gov/state-governor
https://www.congress.gov/state-legislature-web

Write your State Leader Today!

MEET YOUR STATE LEADERS

Our community and state have leaders who solve problems and make decision for us.

- Governor
- State Senator
- State Representative

DESIGN YOUR STATE FLAG

Design Your State Flag:

Federal Government Adventure

Congress: Senators and Representatives make laws.
The President: Leads our country.
The Supreme Court: Interprets the laws.

Virtual tours are fun!

Virtual Tours

The White House
1600 Pennsylvania Avenue., N.W.,
Washington, DC 20500
Email: comments@whitehouse.gov
Website: https://www.whitehouse

Explore important civic places from home with these family-friendly virtual experiences.

White House 360 Virtual Tour:
www.whitehousehistory.org/tour-the-white-house-in-60-degrees

US Capitol Virtual Classroom
www.visitthecapitol.gov/virtual-classroom

Architect of the Capitol - Distance Learning and Virtual Tours
www.aoc.gov/about-us/news-notices

Federal Adventure

How to Contact Your Federal Government

Ways to Learn About Federal Leaders

https://www.usa.gov/federal-agencies

- The President
- Vice President
- U.S. Senators
- U.S. Representatives
- Federal Agencies
- Departments (Education, Health, Transportation, etc.)

Find Your Members of Congress

Search by ZIP code:
https://www.congress.gov\mmbers/find-your-member

Family Action Step

Write to your U.S. Senator or Representative today!

MEET YOUR NATIONAL LEADERS

The President leads our country. Senators and Representatives work in Congress.

President:

U.S. Senator:

U.S. Representative:

BRANCHES OF GOVERNMENT TREE

EXECUTIVE

Write what this branch does:

LEGISLATIVE

Write what this branch does:

JUDICIAL

Write what this branch does:

Community in Action

Today, our family helped our community! When we work together, we make our neighborhood a better place. There are many ways to help – keeping parks clean, helping neighbors, or joining community events.

Our Family Civic Pledge

Sample Pledge: "We promise to stay informed, help others, and build a stronger community."

Now write your own family pledge:

....

....

....

CIVIC EXPLORER AWARD

Awarded to:

....

For learning about government and helping our community!

....

Signature:

Date: ....

Parent & Educator Resource Page

'Civic Adventures' is meant to inspire children to learn about government and community: Here are some ways to continue the conversation and encourage civic-minddedness.

- Ask your child what they'd do if they were in charge!
- Check out books, shows, and movies about community leadership.
- Talk about current events in a child-friendly way.
- Participate in local volunteer activities.

Parent & Educator Resource Page

Parent Tip: Draw a picture to say what matters to your family.

History Task: How our Constitution was written.

Family Task: Visit your senator's or representative's website. What issues do they talk about most?

Closing Message

"Know your purpose. Set out to reach your maximum potential, but do so with the objective of being in service to others."

— Shawntel D. Carey, 2020

From Words to Live By: Quotes by Shawntel D Carey

About the Author

Shawntel D. Carey, MPA, is an entrepreneur and public servant who has dedicated her career to building stronger communities through leadership, education, and service.

She believes that everyone, especially families and children, deserve the knowledge and encouragement to make a positive impact where they live.

www.ingramcontent.com/pod-product-compliance
Lightning Source LLC
Chambersburg PA
CBHW061159030426
42337CB00003B/49